Original title:
A Frosty Glow

Author: Kaido Väinamäe
ISBN HARDBACK: 978-9916-79-351-0
ISBN PAPERBACK: 978-9916-79-352-7
ISBN EBOOK: 978-9916-79-353-4

# The Glint of Winter's Kiss

The frost spreads wide on the ground,
A silvery quilt, beauty found.
Beneath the trees, the whispers gleam,
In quiet nights, the world will dream.

The moonlight dances on the snow,
Each flake a star, a gentle glow.
The air is crisp, a chilling sigh,
As winter's breath drifts softly by.

From window panes, the light refracts,
Crafted patterns, nature acts.
The silence sings, the stillness reigns,
With every breath, the magic gains.

In shadows long, the cold prevails,
A tapestry of winter trails.
The hearth aglow, a refuge warm,
Against the chill, a steadfast charm.

As twilight falls, the colors fade,
Yet in this peace, no need for shade.
Embrace the chill, let heartbeats kiss,
In winter's grasp, we find our bliss.

## Frozen Luster

Ice crystals glimmer bright,
Under the moon's soft light.
A world wrapped in stillness,
Whispers of winter's chill.

Every branch dressed in white,
Sparkling in the night.
Nature's frozen splendor,
A breathtaking, silent tale.

Footprints crunch in the deep,
Secrets that winter keeps.
Through valleys and hills wide,
The luster of frost does bide.

Snowflakes dance in the air,
With beauty beyond compare.
A shimmer on every face,
Inviting us to embrace.

As daylight softly fades,
In shades of silver wades.
Frozen moments cherished,
In this winter's embrace, we flourished.

## Glacial Gaze

Beneath a sky so gray,
Ice fields stretch and sway.
A harsh but lovely sight,
Where day blends into night.

Mountains clad in white,
Stand guard with all their might.
Reflecting time and space,
In nature's cold embrace.

A glacial breath so still,
Calming every thrill.
Winds whisper secrets old,
In tones both sharp and bold.

Voices of the frost,
In shadows, we are lost.
Each step a thrill, a freeze,
In this landscape that appease.

We stand in awe and gaze,
Through winter's frozen maze.
In the icy heart's glow,
The world begins to slow.

# Winter's Whisper

In the hush of night's shroud,
Winter speaks soft and loud.
Crystalline air surrounds,
A harmony of sounds.

Frost blankets every tree,
A sight so pure and free.
Whispers of snowflakes fall,
Nature's soft-spoken call.

Moments lost in the frost,
In this season, we are tossed.
Each breath a cloud of white,
Dance beneath the pale light.

Crisp air sings of the past,
In memories that last.
Through valleys made of dreams,
Echoing winter's themes.

In every flake's descent,
A promise, a sweet scent.
Winter's whispers enfold,
A story gently told.

# Shimmering Frost

Morning breaks with a glow,
Fields of shimmering snow.
A canvas of pure white,
Beneath the sun's warm light.

Each blade of grass aglow,
In the frosty tableau.
Nature's art displayed vast,
In beauty unsurpassed.

Frost kisses every leaf,
Painting dreams beyond belief.
Sparkling jewels abound,
In silence, peace is found.

The air is crisp and clear,
Winter's magic draws near.
Moments freeze in delight,
As day gives way to night.

So let us take a pause,
In wonderment, because,
In this magical gloss,
We find joy in the frost.

# Aurora's Embrace

Dancing lights in the sky,
Wrapped in colors so bright,
Whispers of night draw nigh,
As dawn breaks with new light.

Snowflakes twirl in the air,
Caught in the gentle breeze,
A moment pure and rare,
Nature's soft, sweet tease.

Mountains bathed in gold hue,
Silhouettes against the dawn,
Every shade feels so new,
As shadows gently yawn.

Hearts rejoice in the glow,
A canvas dreamt and spun,
In harmony they flow,
Until the night is done.

Embraced by dawn's soft kiss,
We stand in tranquil grace,
A fleeting, sweetened bliss,
In Aurora's warm embrace.

## Ethereal Winter's Breath

In quiet woods so deep,
Winter breathes soft and slow,
Trees don their crystal keep,
Blanketed in pure snow.

Frosted leaves whisper tales,
Of nights beneath the stars,
A hush as silence hails,
The beauty that is ours.

Moonlit paths shine like dreams,
Crystals glimmer on high,
Each step, a breath that beams,
Underneath the cold sky.

The chill bites but brings peace,
In the stillness we bask,
Winter's beauty won't cease,
In a frosted white mask.

Ethereal moments glide,
As nature curls in rest,
In this wintry, pure ride,
We find our winter's best.

## Radiant Icicles

Hanging from rooftops bright,
Icicles gleam in the sun,
Reflecting purest light,
Winter's art has begun.

In solitude they sway,
Glistening with each soft breeze,
A wondrous, cold ballet,
Nature's frozen decrees.

They shimmer near the eaves,
Pointing towards the vast sky,
Like something that believes,
In magic drawing nigh.

As seasons shift and change,
They melt to nourish anew,
In cycles, endless, strange,
Where life is born from dew.

Radiant, hanging clear,
These crystal tears invite,
To cherish what is near,
In the warmth of delight.

## Shivering Starshine

Beneath the cloak of night,
Stars twinkle, small and bright,
Whispers of dreams take flight,
In the stillness, delight.

A blanket cold and wide,
Wraps the world in soft sighs,
Guiding the moon's proud ride,
Through the dark velvet skies.

Frozen fields glisten white,
Echoes of a deep chill,
In the fading twilight,
Magic lingers, yet still.

Hearts beat in time with glow,
Each shimmer tells a tale,
Of love that starts to grow,
Across the winter trail.

Shivering under light,
We dance in cosmic streams,
In the warmth found tonight,
Living each dream of dreams.

# Chilling Radiance

The moon hangs low in silent night,
Casting shadows, soft and white.
Whispers of frost dance in the air,
Enchanting dreams that linger there.

Branches shimmer, adorned in pearls,
While the world hums, nature twirls.
A silver glow that calms the mind,
In winter's grip, peace we find.

Footsteps crunch on frozen ground,
Where secrets of the night abound.
Each breath a cloud, the world stands still,
As time flows gently, against our will.

Winter's breath, a crystal kiss,
In this realm of frosty bliss.
With every moment, magic grows,
In chilling radiance, beauty flows.

## Icebound Dreams

A landscape cloaked in frosty white,
Where dreams are woven through the night.
Silent echoes in the icy air,
Whispers of wishes, held with care.

Stars above twinkle like jewels,
Guiding hearts, breaking old rules.
Frozen lakes reflect the skies,
In icebound dreams, the spirit flies.

Gentle winds, they softly play,
On fields of snow, they dance and sway.
Each flake a story, unique, divine,
In this chill, our souls entwine.

The world stretches, wrapped in peace,
As moments linger, never cease.
From dusk till dawn, the magic beams,
In the hush of icebound dreams.

# Ethereal Chill

In the early dawn, the world awakes,
With glimmers of light, the stillness breaks.
A veil of frost covers every blade,
In ethereal chill, beauty is laid.

Gentle whispers, a tranquil sound,
As nature's wonders, all around.
Clouds drift slowly, the sun rises,
Unveiling secrets in its surprises.

Footprints trace the snowy path,
As laughter echoes, a joyous math.
With every step, life unfolds,
In the embrace where magic holds.

Crisp air dances through the trees,
A symphony of winter's ease.
Each moment cherished, soft and still,
In this realm of ethereal chill.

# Glistening Crystals

A tapestry of ice, finely spun,
Underneath the warmth of the sun.
Sparkling gems in a sea of white,
Glistening crystals, a pure delight.

Each flake unique, a work of art,
Frosted wonders that touch the heart.
Through silver branches, shadows play,
In nature's gallery, night and day.

Whispers of winter on the breeze,
A chilling serenade through the trees.
A moment captured, forever gleams,
In the beauty of glistening dreams.

As twilight falls, the magic swells,
Where each soft echo of winter dwells.
With every breath, the world ignites,
In glistening crystals, purest lights.

## Glimmer of the Frozen Realm

In the stillness of the night,
Snowflakes whisper soft and light,
Underneath the pale moon's gaze,
Magic twinkles, softly sways.

Trees dressed in icicles bright,
Glowing softly, pure delight,
Footsteps crunching on the path,
Nature's peace, a quiet bath.

Starlit skies embrace the ground,
A world cloaked, so profound,
Frosted breath, the air is cold,
Stories of the winter told.

Each glimmer, a tale untold,
In the cold, hearts won't grow old,
Wonders wrapped in winter's veil,
Glimmers shine and never fail.

Softly, secrets drift away,
In the frozen realm we stay,
Embracing all the winter's schemes,
We awaken from our dreams.

## Sparkling Frost on Twilight's Edge

As daylight dims and shadows blend,
Sparkling frost begins to send,
Glimmers bright on every leaf,
Nature's beauty, pure and brief.

Twilight whispers, colors blend,
Rays of orange, pinks descend,
Each branch glistens, crystals near,
A fleeting moment to revere.

The chill of night begins to creep,
In silent woods where spirits sleep,
Each breath visible in the dark,
While the stars ignite a spark.

Time stands still on twilight's edge,
In the stillness, a solemn pledge,
To treasure every fleeting sight,
As day surrenders into night.

Underneath the twilight skies,
Magic dances, softly lies,
In the glow of evening's head,
Sparkling frost on twilight's edge.

# Crystalized Silence

In the hush of winter's night,
Crystalized silence feels so right,
Every echo wrapped in snow,
Whispers soft, in gentle flow.

Nature pauses, takes a breath,
In this stillness, there's no death,
Muffled sounds, the world retreats,
In the quiet, heartbeats meet.

Frosty windows, dreams awake,
Silent wishes softly break,
Stars above, like diamonds glow,
Guiding paths where cold winds blow.

In the depth of tranquil lanes,
Echoes of the night remain,
Feel the chill, the peace surrounds,
In crystal silence, love abounds.

As dawn approaches, light will rise,
Breaking quiet with warm skies,
Yet in our hearts this stillness stays,
A crystalized silence in our days.

## Luminous Winter's Dance

Underneath a sky of grey,
Winter whispers, dances sway,
Snowflakes twirl in pure delight,
Luminous in soft moonlight.

Branches bow with icy grace,
Wind's embrace, a fleeting chase,
Nature's steps upon the ground,
In this waltz, pure joy is found.

Footprints tracing through the snow,
In this dance, we come and go,
Twinkling lights adorn the night,
Every moment feels so right.

Luminous, the night unfolds,
A winter's tale, forever told,
With each flurry, hearts ignite,
In this dance, we find the light.

As dawn breaks and day is born,
Memories of night adorn,
In winter's arms, we twirl and prance,
Forever held in winter's dance.

# Prismatic Frost

Awake in the morning light,
Frost paints the world so bright.
Colors dance on crystal blades,
Nature's art, a dream cascades.

Each breath whispers of the chill,
Patterns formed by winter's will.
A tapestry of silver hues,
In the quiet, beauty brews.

Sunrise glints on frozen lakes,
Echoes of the beauty makes.
Reflecting visions, pure and clear,
In the stillness, magic near.

Beneath the branches, shadows play,
Frosty jewels greet the day.
A landscape wrapped in icy threads,
Whispers of white, where winter treads.

As evening falls, the world aglow,
Prismatic lights begin to flow.
In the cold, a warmth so sweet,
Frosty wonders at our feet.

## Gentle Crystal Caress

Softly falls the winter's breath,
Whispering tales of quiet death.
Each flake a feathered lullaby,
In the hush, the world sighs by.

Gentle hands of frost extend,
Caressing earth, as day can bend.
A cloak of white, serene and pure,
In this stillness, hearts endure.

Beneath the moonlight's tender gaze,
Crystal shards in a silver haze.
Nature's jewels scattered wide,
A tranquil beauty, winter's pride.

As shadows stretch, the night will wake,
A shimmering glow, the cold will stake.
In each moment, a quiet bliss,
Kissed by frost in nature's kiss.

Awakening as dawn appears,
The world adorned with frozen tears.
Gentle crystal, a silent song,
In every heartbeat, we belong.

# Chilled Illuminations

In the depths of winter's reach,
Chilled illuminations teach.
Stars above in icy night,
Guide us through the silvery light.

Night unfolds with gentle grace,
Frosty breath on every face.
Each moment, a glimmer bright,
Holds the magic of the night.

Trees adorned with nature's lace,
Glistening diamonds in their place.
Whispers of the frozen air,
A world transformed, beyond compare.

Shimmering paths that light the way,
In soft glow, the night will stay.
Every shadow cloaked in white,
Wrapped in chill, we find our flight.

As dawn breaks and stars retreat,
Softly fades the icy sleet.
Chilled illuminations fade,
Yet in memory, they cascade.

# A Glint in the Deep Freeze

Beneath the layers, silence grips,
A glint in the deep freeze slips.
Echoes quiet, voices small,
In the stillness, we hear it all.

Glittering specks on snowflakes dance,
Captured light in a fleeting chance.
Every moment, a story unfolds,
In the cold, the whisper unfolds.

Frigid air cradles hopes untold,
In frozen realms, the brave and bold.
A glint shines where shadows deepen,
In the night, our spirits steepen.

Twilight's arms embrace the chill,
Nurturing dreams that winter will fill.
A flash of warmth, a promise near,
In the deep freeze, hearts revere.

As twilight fades to morning's glow,
The glint reminds us, time will flow.
In every flake and every breeze,
Exists a spark, a heart at ease.

# Icy Radiance

In the still of night, stars gleam bright,
Cold winds whisper secrets of frost,
A silver moon with a gentle light,
In beauty's grip, the warmth is lost.

Crystals dance on the frozen ground,
Each step a tale of winter's breath,
Nature's art in silence found,
A fleeting dream, kissed by death.

Glimmers trapped in branches bare,
A world transformed in pale delight,
Magic lingers in the frosty air,
Wrapped in the cloak of endless night.

Whispers of ice in the darkened trees,
Holding secrets of what was before,
Each moment hangs like a fragile breeze,
A shiver that reaches to the core.

Icy radiance, a shimmering sight,
A canvas brushed in silver and blue,
Nature's beauty in the quiet night,
A glow that speaks of the cold and true.

## Glimmering Crystals

Frozen jewels are scattered wide,
Glimmers wink in morning's light,
Nature's treasure, vast with pride,
A symphony of pure delight.

Each crystal holds a story dear,
Captured moments of winter's breath,
In their shine, we see and hear,
Life in stillness, a dance with death.

Branches sway, adorned in white,
Fractals branch in pleasing forms,
In this realm, pure magic bright,
Where nature's grace, a spirit warms.

Twinkling snowflakes drift and sway,
A glittering blanket hugs the ground,
Translucent dreams in brilliant array,
In every flake, lost joys are found.

Glimmering crystals, fleeting and fair,
Guardians of winter's soft embrace,
A glittering world beyond compare,
In their light, we find our place.

## Winter's Whispering Light

In the hush of snow, whispers glide,
Winter's breath in a soft embrace,
Gentle chill rests by my side,
In every shadow, I find grace.

Trees wear coats of sparkling white,
The heart of night beats steady, slow,
Underneath the luminous flight,
Arise the dreams that winter know.

Silvery paths reflect the stars,
Footsteps softly kiss the ground,
In this stillness, forget the scars,
Peace resides where hope is found.

Frosted air, a tapestry fine,
Woven threads of dreams untold,
In the light, a world divine,
Winter's story begins to unfold.

Winter's whisper carries delight,
In every sigh, the promise grows,
A gentle flicker, soft and bright,
Illuminating the path we chose.

## Shimmering Chill

Beneath the bright and starry sky,
The world is draped in icy lace,
Where whispers hint of dreams nearby,
And shadows dance in silent grace.

Tread lightly on the snowy ways,
The chill wraps tight, a lover's hold,
In fleeting moments, time betrays,
As nature's warmth turns softly cold.

Glints of silver on branches sway,
Echoes of winter's softest breath,
In twilight's glow, the night will play,
With dreams entwined in silent depth.

Hidden dances of the night,
Glimpses of life in frozen streams,
Every corner sparkles bright,
Where visions linger in our dreams.

Shimmering chill stirs hearts anew,
Where magic blankets every hill,
In winter's grasp, the world feels true,
Embraced in beauty, calm and still.

# Frosted Reverie

A blanket white, the world asleep,
In dreams of frost, the silence deep.
Each flake a whisper from the skies,
In winter's hold, the magic lies.

Beneath the ice, the rivers flow,
In frozen time, the secrets grow.
The stars above, they flicker bright,
Guiding souls through the long night.

With every breath, the chill ignites,
A dance of frost, the heart delights.
In shimmering fields, the shadows play,
As night embraces the fading day.

A moment's pause, a fleeting glimpse,
In frozen dreams, the spirit limps.
Yet in the stillness, hope resides,
For spring will come, and time abides.

# Celestial Blush

As twilight falls, the sky ignites,
With shades of rose, the day invites.
The stars awaken, one by one,
In hues of magic, night begun.

A breath of wind, a soft caress,
The universe in endless dress.
Each twinkling light, a story spun,
A cosmic dance, a heartbeat run.

In shadows deep, the dreams take flight,
With every star, a spark of light.
As moonlit beams on silver seas,
Whisper the tales of ancient trees.

The nightingale sings a lullaby,
To the dreaming world, beneath the sky.
In celestial blush, hearts entwine,
A tapestry of love divine.

# Glacial Whispers

In icy realms where silence reigns,
The whispers echo in snowy plains.
Each breath a cloud in the frosty air,
Tales of old in the chill laid bare.

The glaciers groan with ancient songs,
In time's embrace, where it belongs.
With every crack, a voice unfolds,
In secrets kept by the frozen holds.

Beneath the ice, a life persists,
In starlit dreams, the heart insists.
The world transforms with every thaw,
As nature writes without a flaw.

Eternal dance of frost and flame,
In crystal words, we chant the name.
Of beauty found in stark contrast,
In glacial whispers, forever cast.

## Shivering Light

In dawn's embrace, the shadows fade,
With shivering light, the night's betrayed.
Each ray a brush on cold, damp earth,
Awakening life, igniting birth.

The trees reach high, the branches sway,
In morning's glow, they find their way.
As dew-drop jewels on petals gleam,
Unveiling nature's sweetest dream.

The sun will rise, a fiery ball,
Its warmth will chase the shadows small.
In every glint, a promise bright,
In shivering glow, dispelled the night.

And in this dance, the world ignites,
With joy reborn in golden sights.
In every heartbeat, life takes flight,
Through shivering moments, we find light.

# Frost's tender caress

In the quiet of dawn, frost gleams wide,
Nature's blanket, a silvery guide.
Whispers of cold, the world holds still,
A gentle touch, a winter's thrill.

Branches adorned with shimmering lace,
Each crystal spark, a delicate trace.
The air bites sharp, yet crisp and sweet,
In this embrace, time feels complete.

Hushed footsteps on a snow-clad ground,
Echoes of peace, in silence found.
Sunrise glimmers, the icy sighs,
As day awakens, winter complies.

A fleeting moment, yet it stays,
In hearts warmed by the frosty gaze.
Memories linger, soft and bright,
Cradled in arms of winter's light.

## Shivers of Light

Dancing shadows in the fading glow,
Whispers of warmth in the winter's snow.
Glistening beams through the branches peek,
Nature's spectacle, serene and sleek.

Evening cools, the colors blend,
A canvas of twilight, as day does end.
Stars awaken, like jewels in flight,
A shimmering promise of endless night.

Crisp air tinkles, a soft refrain,
Every moment, a gentle gain.
Under the moon, dreams softly soar,
Shivers of light, forevermore.

The world transforms in luminous grace,
Each flicker reveals a hidden space.
Boundless wonders, in silence shared,
In the heart of winter, love declared.

# Winter's Caress

Snowflakes twirl, a ballet divine,
Whispering secrets, so soft, so fine.
Every flake, unique in descent,
A fleeting touch, a chill well-spent.

Underneath the hush, the earth dreams,
Frozen rivers, glistening streams.
Branches arch as if in prayer,
Embracing the cold, a wild affair.

Breath misting in the frosty air,
Moments unfurl, stripped of despair.
Winter's caress, a soothing balm,
In nature's grasp, we find our calm.

Colors muted, yet they still glow,
In the heart's warmth, love does flow.
Each icy gust brings whispers clear,
In winter's arms, we conquer fear.

## Ethereal Breezes

Curled in the night, soft whispers sigh,
Ethereal breezes drift and fly.
Through the trees, they echo a song,
A lullaby where shadows belong.

Cool winds weave through the sleeping leaves,
Bringing solace, as daylight grieves.
Each breath of air, a gentle tease,
In the dark, we find our ease.

Stars above, like diamonds shine,
Bathed in whispers, the world aligns.
Every heartbeat, every dream,
Carried along in the moon's soft beam.

In the quiet, a promise waits,
Ethereal breezes, the heart's gates.
Awakening hope, as shadows play,
In winter's embrace, we find our way.

## Frost-Kissed Serenade


Whispers dance on frosty air,
Each breath a cloud, delicate and rare.
Nature sleeps beneath a quilt,
A dream of white where time stands still.

Branches bow with icy grace,
Crystals shimmering, a tranquil space.
Underneath the silent sky,
Winter's serenade, a gentle sigh.

Moonlight spills on frozen streams,
Reflecting softly, like silver dreams.
Footsteps muffled, echoes fade,
In this stillness, memories made.

Stars peek out, a twinkling show,
Night wraps all in its soft glow.
A world transformed, pure and bright,
In this frost-kissed serenade of night.

## Luminous Frostbite

In the heart of winter's hold,
A tale of frost and whispers told.
Each flake, a tiny work of art,
Frostbite ignites the beating heart.

Icicles dangle, sharp and clear,
Nature's jewels, beautiful yet sheer.
Breath visible on the coldest eve,
A moment captured, hard to believe.

Softly falling, the snowflakes drift,
Painting the world as nature's gift.
Every shimmer in the pale moonlight,
A luminous dance, a stunning sight.

Trees are cloaked in crystal shells,
A frozen realm where beauty dwells.
Whispers of winter, gentle and bright,
Luminous frostbite, pure delight.

# Glacial Glisten

Underneath a sky of gray,
The world transforms, the colors fray.
Glaciers glow with a timeless grace,
Nature's wonder, a frozen place.

Rivers halt in a crystal flow,
A world entranced in winter's show.
Each crevice shines in icy gleam,
Glacial towers, a frosty dream.

Silent shadows play on white,
In the quiet of the night.
Footprints trace the glistening ground,
Echoes of life, serene, profound.

Snow drapes o'er the sleeping trees,
As if wrapped in a soft, cool breeze.
Time stands still, a moment to pause,
In glacial glisten, nature's cause.

## Twilight's Icy Touch

As twilight falls, the chill sets in,
A whisper beckons, where dreams begin.
Frost paints the edges of each leaf,
In delicate beauty, a moment brief.

The sky blushes with a pastel hue,
Stars awaken, the night's debut.
Silent and soft, the shadows creep,
In twilight's touch, the world falls asleep.

Moonbeams dance on the frozen lake,
Ripples twinkle, a gentle wake.
A hush surrounds, a gentle trance,
In icy touch, the night begins its dance.

Frost-kissed air, a tender sigh,
Embraced by silence, the time flies by.
Beneath the stars, a story spins,
In twilight's icy touch, where magic begins.

# The Shimmering Haze

In the golden embrace of dawn,
Shadows dance on the lawn.
Whispers weave through the trees,
A soft sigh on the breeze.

Colors blend in a soft ballet,
As night gives way to day.
Dewdrops glisten like pearls,
Painting dreams in soft swirls.

A world dressed in light's attire,
Each moment sparks with fire.
Nature twirls in pure delight,
Basking in the morning light.

Echoes of laughter take flight,
Banishing the veil of night.
With every heartbeat, it grows,
A tale that the universe knows.

In this shimmering haze so fine,
Life breathes, dances, divine.
Every ray holds a spark of grace,
In this enchanted space.

# Frosted Echoes

Beneath the veil of winter's chill,
Whispers linger, time stands still.
Frosted patterns on the glass,
Nature's art, a perfect pass.

A hush falls soft on the ground,
Where stillness is the only sound.
Footprints trace a silent arc,
Leading into the stark.

Trees wear coats of shimmering white,
Under the glow of pale moonlight.
Every flake tells a story near,
Echoes of warmth in the frosty air.

Lamp posts glow with a golden hue,
Shadows stretch as the night bids adieu.
Chimes of laughter dance and glide,
In winter's embrace, we confide.

Frosted echoes fill the night,
Starlit dreams take their flight.
In every breath, a chill we chase,
Finding warmth in this frost-kissed space.

# Crystalized Dusk

When the sun dips low, colors blend,
A tapestry where day meets end.
Shadows stretch across the lane,
Every corner holds a gain.

Clouds painted with a rosy hue,
Stirring dreams, both old and new.
Whispers of night softly call,
As daylight begins to fall.

The horizon glows, a fleeting kiss,
On the cusp of dark, a gentle bliss.
Stars awaken, twinkling bright,
Guiding wanderers in the night.

From dusk's embrace, possibilities unfold,
Stories woven, brave and bold.
Within the depths of serene night,
Lies the heart's beginning flight.

In this crystalized dusk so fair,
Dreams take form, floating in air.
As night descends with a soft embrace,
A dance of time, in its space.

# Charmed in Ice

In a glen where silence reigns,
Nature's magic softly gains.
Icicles hang like crystal beads,
Whispers carried on gentle seeds.

A kingdom draped in frosty lace,
Every corner, a sparkling face.
Moonlight glimmers on the stream,
Painting winter's waking dream.

Footsteps crunch on the silver snow,
Frosted branches gently bow low.
The world is held in a tender trance,
A silent song, a frozen dance.

Stars twinkle like gems in the night,
Casting spells in the pale light.
Within this wonder, wild and free,
Life finds a way to simply be.

Charmed in ice, we lose our fears,
Embraced in enchantment, through the years.
In every flake, we find a trace,
Of dreams that blossom in this space.

# Shaded Brilliance

In wooded halls where sunlight bends,
The shadows dance, the magic blends.
Leaves whisper tales of ancient lore,
A quiet peace, forevermore.

Beneath the arch of emerald trees,
A soft caress in summer's breeze.
Colors swirl in patterns bright,
Nature's canvas, pure delight.

In hidden glades where secrets lie,
Birds sing sweetly, spirits fly.
With every step, the heart shall soar,
In shaded brilliance, we explore.

When twilight casts its golden hues,
The fireflies light the paths we choose.
A fleeting glimpse, a fleeting chance,
In nature's nocturnal dance.

So wander forth, let beauty reign,
In every corner, joy remain.
For in the woods, we find our way,
In shaded brilliance, day by day.

# The Cool Embrace

Upon the shores where waters play,
The ocean whispers night and day.
With every wave, the soft caress,
A cool embrace, a sweet caress.

The salty breeze, it fills the air,
A soothing balm, beyond compare.
Seagulls dance on sunlight's beam,
In this moment, we can dream.

With every tide, a heartbeat flows,
The rhythm of life, it ebbs and grows.
And in the calm, we find our peace,
In nature's arms, our worries cease.

The horizon glows, a colorful show,
As day gives way to twilight's glow.
Beneath the stars, our spirits race,
All wrapped in the cool embrace.

So let us linger, let us stay,
In love with life, come what may.
For in the night, our dreams take flight,
In this cool embrace, all feels right.

# Radiant Snowflakes

Fluttering down from skies so gray,
Snowflakes fall in a magical ballet.
Each one unique, a wondrous sight,
Radiant beauty, pure and white.

They blanket the earth in soft repose,
A world transformed, as stillness grows.
Whispers of winter kiss the air,
In frosted wonder, we feel the care.

The laughter echoes, children play,
Building dreams in a snowy display.
With every flake, our hearts embrace,
The shining wonder, a serene grace.

As twilight falls, the moonlight beams,
Upon the snow, it sparkles, gleams.
In this quiet, a magic stirs,
The world enchanted, as winter purrs.

So let us wander through the night,
As snowflakes dance in silver light.
In winter's arms, we find our way,
Radiant snowflakes, here to stay.

## Icy Serenade

In the chill of winter's breath,
A symphony of life and death.
Frosted branches, a crystal crown,
Nature's music, soft and profound.

Through the stillness, silence reigns,
An icy serenade, sweet refrains.
With every note, a shiver sings,
The frost, the whispers, the joy it brings.

Beneath the stars, the world asleep,
While shadows dance and secrets keep.
The night unfolds its frosty cloak,
With whispered dreams, the world awoke.

Wrapped in warmth, we cherish still,
The icy wonders, the winter chill.
For in the cold, we find our grace,
In icy serenades, we embrace.

So let us wander hand in hand,
Through glistening fields of crystal land.
For in the night, our hearts shall sway,
In icy serenade, we'll stay.

# Cubic Adornments

In the frame of glowing light,
Cubes of color, shining bright.
Artistry in every sway,
Nature's gems in grand array.

Frozen whispers in the air,
Charmed by shapes beyond compare.
Each a story, a delight,
Crafted visions, pure and right.

Layers deep, the brilliance weaves,
Tales of wonder, it conceives.
Every edge, a dance of fate,
Cubic wonders captivate.

As the shadows softly play,
All around, the hues display.
In their silence, secrets bloom,
Adornments bright, dispel the gloom.

Fragments catch the dawn's first glow,
In their presence, dreams can grow.
Weave them close, this magical art,
Cubic adornments, joy impart.

# Serene Icebound Gleam

Silent waters, crystal blue,
Mirrored skies reflect the hue.
In the stillness, peace is found,
Echoes soft, a soothing sound.

Snowflakes dance like fleeting dreams,
Weaving through the icy streams.
Glistening with a gentle grace,
Nature's beauty, time's embrace.

Beneath the frost, the earth sleeps tight,
Bathed in silver, purest light.
Veils of white, a soft array,
Serene moments mark the day.

In the twilight, shadows creep,
Wrapped in silence, still, and deep.
A tranquil heart, a quiet scream,
Life unfolds in this serene dream.

Morning breaks with hues so bright,
Colors clash in wondrous fight.
Yet within this vibrant seam,
Lies the calm of icebound gleam.

# Mysterious Shards of Light

Cascading rays through branches weave,
Mysteries in shadows breathe.
Every shard, a tale untold,
Reflections dance, bright and bold.

Glistening paths on autumn leaves,
Nature whispers, heart believes.
Light and dark in soft embrace,
Chasing thoughts in hidden space.

Fractured beams, they shine and fade,
In the forest, dreams invade.
Each scoop of light, a spark ignites,
Within the depths of starry nights.

Colors merge, then swirl away,
A fleeting moment, here to stay.
In the depths, a heart takes flight,
Boundless wonders, sharp and bright.

With each glimmer, secrets blend,
Cascading tales that twist and bend.
In the silence, hear the night,
Guardians of the shards of light.

# Illuminated Winter's Veil

Frosted breath in morning's chill,
Nature's canvas, pure and still.
Whispers weave through fluffy snow,
Illuminated paths below.

Silver hues on branches lie,
Stars like diamonds in the sky.
Every flake a crafted gem,
In this world, we find our hem.

Footprints tracing stories there,
Hidden echoes in the air.
With each step, the past will tell,
Dance upon this winter's spell.

Glistening skies, twilight's grace,
In the silence, we embrace.
Wrapped in warmth, beneath the star,
Winter's veil, we wander far.

As the night brings comfort near,
Hearts entwined with love and cheer.
In this realm, together we sail,
Lost in peace, illuminated veil.

# Wintry Luminance

In the hush of falling snow,
Twinkling lights begin to glow,
Whispers of a winter night,
Casting shadows, pure and bright.

Glistening on the frozen trees,
Dancing gently with the breeze,
Every flake a work of art,
Warming softly every heart.

Blankets wrap the world in white,
Covering earth in quiet light,
Moonbeams play on icy streams,
Harmonizing with our dreams.

Stars above, a twinkling show,
Guiding pathways through the snow,
Magic lingers in the air,
As we find our joys to share.

In the beauty of this freeze,
Nature whispers, if you please,
Take a moment, breathe it in,
Feel the peace, let joy begin.

# Sparkling Veil

Draped in silver, soft and light,
Veils of mist in morning bright,
Each drop glistening in the sun,
Whispers of the day begun.

Colors dance in dew-kissed grass,
As the moments slowly pass,
Nature's jewels on display,
Crowning beauty of the day.

Gentle breezes bring a sigh,
Carrying dreams that float on high,
Every shimmer, every gleam,
Painting visions, waking dream.

Softly now, the world awakes,
Life returns, the stillness breaks,
Golden hues embrace the morn,
In this light, we are reborn.

Moments linger, sweet and pure,
Every heartbeat, every cure,
In this sparkling, tender grace,
Find your joy, your sacred space.

## Diamond Dew

Morning light on twilight's edge,
Glistening drops on nature's ledge,
Each one shines like precious stone,
Whispers of the night now flown.

On the petals, soft and round,
Little treasures can be found,
Catch a glimpse, a fleeting sight,
Nature's magic, pure delight.

Waking dreams in every drop,
Making hearts and spirits hop,
In the silence, life unfolds,
Stories waiting to be told.

Giggles dance on morning breeze,
Carrying laughter through the trees,
Diamond dew, a gentle grace,
Wrapping earth in its embrace.

Hold this moment, sweet and real,
Let each droplet help you heal,
In the dawn's soft, glowing hue,
Find your peace in diamond dew.

# Enchanted Frost

When the night lays down its breath,
Frost appears, a quiet death,
Covering the world in charm,
Touching all with frigid calm.

Each blade whispers stories old,
Crystals bright, a tale retold,
In their spark, a secret shared,
Hope and wonder, deeply paired.

Through the trees, the whispers fly,
Frosted branches reaching high,
Nature's voice, a lullaby,
Softly sung beneath the sky.

As the dawn begins to break,
Sunlight warms, the frost can shake,
But the magic, Touched and lost,
Leaves us longing for the frost.

Keep this beauty in your heart,
Let it glow, a work of art,
In the stillness, find your way,
In enchanted frost, we stay.

# A Shiver of Wonder

In twilight's warm embrace, we stand,
Hearts racing at the unknown land.
Stars twinkle like jewels from afar,
In silence, we discover who we are.

Each breath a canvas of icy mist,
Moments unfold, not one is missed.
The night whispers secrets, soft and low,
In every shadow, wonders glow.

We dance in the light of a silver moon,
Nature's refrain, a gentle tune.
With every step, the world unfolds,
Mysteries alive, waiting to be told.

The skies paint stories in shades of gray,
Guiding our hearts along the way.
Every shiver sparks a new delight,
In this wondrous tapestry of night.

In every glance, a spark ignites,
A shiver of magic in the heights.
Together we wander through endless skies,
With wonder reflecting in our eyes.

# Frost-fringed Horizons

Beneath the pale and frosty glow,
Horizons stretch where cold winds blow.
With every step, the world transforms,
Nature wraps life in shimmering forms.

The air is crisp, a breath of dreams,
Echoing softly in silent streams.
Frost-kissed branches in morning light,
Whisper the secrets of the night.

Mountains stand tall, draped in white,
Guardians of awe, a breathtaking sight.
Footprints follow trails untold,
Into realms where the brave are bold.

Each sigh of wind carries tales of old,
In the icy embrace, their stories unfold.
Glimmers of sun on frost-crusted ground,
A treasure of beauty waiting to be found.

Frost-fringed horizons beckon our hearts,
Inviting us forth, where adventure starts.
In every glimmer of the frozen dawn,
Dreams awaken as shadows are drawn.

## Frozen Melodies

A symphony plays in the winter's hush,
Notes dance lightly in a gentle rush.
Crystal flakes fall, a delicate song,
In this frozen world, we all belong.

Each twinkle of ice, a musical chime,
Echoes of beauty, transcending time.
The trees hum softly, their branches sway,
In the heart of winter, where spirits play.

Footsteps crunch on a tapestry white,
A rhythm of joy in the soft moonlight.
Whispers of frost weave through the night,
Creating a wonder, pure and bright.

The air tingles, alive with sound,
In the still of the night, magic abounds.
As melodies rise with each gentle breeze,
Nature's orchestra brings us to our knees.

Frozen melodies fill the air,
A reminder of life's beauty, rare.
In every note, the essence of grace,
Winter's serenade, a warm embrace.

# Whispers of the Cold

In the quiet of winter, whispers call,
Echoing softly, touching us all.
The breath of the earth, a frosty sigh,
In shadows where secrets quietly lie.

Blankets of snow wrapped tight around,
Warmth of the hearth in silence is found.
Stories of warmth flicker like flame,
Lost in the cold, but never the same.

Each gust of wind carries words unseen,
Echoing softly where dreams have been.
The night holds promise, wrapped in frost,
In the beauty of stillness, we find what's lost.

With each falling snowflake, a kiss from above,
Whispers of nature, a testament of love.
In every moment, the world holds tight,
To the magic of winter, cloaked in light.

As dawn breaks softly, whispers remain,
In the heart of the cold, joy mingles with pain.
We listen closely, to tales yet untold,
In the breath of the winter, we find our bold.

# Chilling Brilliance


Upon the frozen lake it gleams,
A crystal world where silence dreams.
Stars flicker in the moonlit sky,
Whispers of winter's soft goodbye.

The icy breath of night unfurls,
Soft flurries dance and twirl like pearls.
In the stillness, hearts ignite,
With chilling brilliance in the night.

Rustling branches, cloaked in white,
Embrace the calm of winter's light.
Each breath a cloud, a fleeting ghost,
A moment's peace that we can boast.

Frost-kissed windows frame the view,
Nature paints a world anew.
In every flake, a story lies,
Each one unique as it flies.

So let us wander, hand in hand,
Through this enchanting, snow-clad land.
With chilling brilliance all around,
In winter's magic we are bound.

## Snowy Lightshow

The world transformed in glowing light,
A snowy canvas, soft and bright.
Beneath the stars, the snowflakes fall,
A shimmering dance that enchants all.

Moonbeams sparkle on the snow,
A gentle touch, a soft glow.
In the hush, the night unfolds,
A snowy lightshow, a tale retold.

Frosty branches catch the gleam,
Illuminated in a dream.
The laughter of the chilly breeze,
A symphony that sets hearts at ease.

Footprints trail in patterns fine,
Stories linger in each line.
Whispers of nature softly play,
As night surrenders to the day.

In this winter wonderland,
We find the joy of life at hand.
A snowy lightshow, pure and bright,
Guides our hearts through the long night.

# Winter's Silvery Veil

A silver hush upon the ground,
In winter's silvery veil, we're found.
Quiet moments, soft and pure,
In this stillness, hearts endure.

The air is crisp with frosty breath,
A peaceful calm, a dance with death.
Each tree a statue, proud and tall,
Wrapped in white, a wondrous thrall.

Snowflakes tumble, softly land,
Nature's touch, a gentle hand.
We gather close, 'neath the stars' embrace,
Finding warmth in this cold space.

With every step, the world transforms,
In winter's grip, the heart warms.
A sparkling quilt, a dreamlike tale,
Awaits us in this silvery veil.

Together we marvel, hand in hand,
In a breathtaking, snowy land.
With winter's chill, our spirits sail,
Forever touched by the silvery veil.

## Frostwine Dreams

In the quiet of the winter night,
Frostwine dreams take silent flight.
Warmed by fire, we sit and share,
Whispers of hopes in the frosty air.

The moon pours silver on the ground,
In stillness, love and joy abound.
Each sip a warmth, a cozy cheer,
Frostwine dreams draw us near.

With every laugh, the shadows play,
In the heart, the cold gives way.
As snowflakes weave their delicate thread,
We toast the moments, memories spread.

Like swirling snow, our thoughts collide,
In freezing chill, we find our guide.
With every glass, our spirits beam,
Lost in the warmth of frostwine dreams.

So let the winter winds embrace,
As we create our joyful space.
In the tapestry of love we schemed,
Together, we find our frostwine dreams.

## Glacial Twilight

In the hush of evening's breath,
The sky shimmers, deep and blue,
A world wrapped in icy velvet,
Whispers secrets, old and true.

Mountains stand like silent guards,
Their peaks kissed by the waning light,
Glistening under pale stars' watch,
Marking the end of day's quiet fight.

Frosted trees weave tales of night,
Each branch draped in crystal lace,
Echoes of the daylight's flight,
A frozen frame, a timeless space.

As shadows lengthen, colors fade,
The glowing moon starts her ascent,
Nature's canvas, slowly laid,
Cradles dreams in cool descent.

In this moment, hearts align,
With the rhythms of the cold,
In glacial twilight, spirits shine,
Finding warmth in stories told.

## Frost-Kissed Dreams

Beneath the blanket of the night,
Whispers dance on frosty air,
Dreams awaken, taking flight,
In the silence, pure and rare.

Stars scatter like glimmering dew,
Each one holding a wish anew,
As shadows play with silver beams,
Embraced by frost, like gentle dreams.

The moon conducts a frosty choir,
While snowflakes drift, soft as sighs,
In this world, both calm and dire,
Life's magic lingers, ever wise.

Underneath the tranquil sky,
Hearts entwined in secret schemes,
In frost-kissed breaths, we sigh,
Nurturing our wildest dreams.

So let us wander, hand in hand,
Through this winter wonderland,
With every step, a story we weave,
In frost-kissed dreams, we believe.

# Luminous Fragments

In the depths of winter's night,
Softly gleam those fragments bright,
Scattered stars in darkened skies,
Whispering through the cold, they rise.

Each glimmer tells a tale untold,
Of warmth and love, of hearts grown bold,
Shattered pieces of the past,
In their glow, we find contrast.

Frozen lakes, like mirrors gleam,
Reflecting hopes and whispered dreams,
Every facet catches light,
In luminous fragments, pure delight.

As night unfolds, our spirits soar,
With every twinkle, we explore,
The beauty found in flickering spark,
Revealing light within the dark.

With a breath, we hold them close,
These luminous fragments, we cherish most,
In the heart of winter's embrace,
We find our home, our sacred place.

## Chilled Luminescence

A quiet glow in frosty air,
Chilled luminescence everywhere,
Glistening on branches bare,
Bringing magic, beyond compare.

Night wraps the earth in gentle gray,
Soft whispers from the stars convey,
In every shimmer, secrets lie,
A buffer 'gainst the cold night's sigh.

The moon's soft touch creates delight,
A guiding hand through velvet night,
Each flake that falls reflects the glow,
Of dreams reaffirmed, and love that flows.

Silence reigns, except for hearts,
Beating softly, as night departs,
In chilled luminescence, we find,
The warmth of souls forever kind.

So let the world around us freeze,
In this chill, our spirits ease,
For wrapped in light, we shall always be,
Together, warm, eternally free.

# Luminous Snowdrift

Soft flakes dance in twilight's glow,
Blanketing the earth below.
Whispers of winter fill the air,
Wrapped in silence everywhere.

Moonlight bathes the silent ground,
In a world where peace is found.
Stars twinkle in the crisp night sky,
As dreams and frost begin to fly.

Branches wear a coat of white,
Sparkling gently in the night.
Each flake tells a silent tale,
Of winter's breath, both soft and pale.

Footprints trace the path of woe,
Upon this glistening snow.
Through the night and into day,
Nature's charm will softly sway.

In this realm, all worries cease,
Finding solace, finding peace.
Luminous snowdrifts warm the heart,
In winter's grasp, we play our part.

## Shining in the Frost

Glistening sparks in morning light,
Every crystal shines so bright.
Frosted grass, a jeweled bed,
Where dreams of winter softly tread.

Nature's brush paints every hue,
Capturing a world so new.
Each breath comes in gentle sighs,
As silver clouds drift through the skies.

Icicles hanging from the eaves,
Whisper tales of winter thieves.
Stealing warmth with every breath,
A dance of life, a waltz with death.

Sunrise warms the chilly morn,
Golden rays where frost was born.
In the glow, the world awakes,
With every shimmer, beauty breaks.

Moments held in frosty hands,
Across the fields and barren lands.
Shining brightly, winter's show,
A fleeting glimpse of nature's glow.

# Frosty Whispers of Dawn

Whispers soft upon the breeze,
As dawn breaks, the world at ease.
Frosty tendrils greet the day,
Nature wakes in shades of gray.

Crimson skies begin to glow,
Painting scenes with twilight's flow.
Every leaf, a crystal gem,
In a world that feels like hem.

Birds take flight in shimmering air,
Dancing free without a care.
Echoes of a nighttime song,
Filling hearts where dreams belong.

Frosty whispers weave their thread,
Through the silence, softly spread.
As the sun climbs higher still,
Life awakens with a thrill.

Moments captured in a flash,
Fleeting seconds, quick as a dash.
Frosty whispers fade away,
As the dawn brings forth the day.

# Icebound Glimmer

In the stillness, shadows play,
As icebound glimmers light the way.
Frozen rivers, a silver stream,
Reflecting all like a waking dream.

Each crystal formed, a masterpiece,
A frozen art that will not cease.
Nature's breath, a chilly sigh,
Underneath the endless sky.

Branches bend with morning's weight,
Crystals catch the early fate.
Shimmering softly, secrets told,
In the chill, the world feels bold.

Winter's heart beats strong and true,
In every hue, in every view.
Fleeting moments hold us tight,
In the dance of day and night.

Icebound glimmers sparkle bright,
A wondrous sight in dawn's first light.
Embrace the cold, the beauty so,
In frozen lands where wonders grow.

## Crystal Glow at Dawn

In the morning's gentle light,
Crystal sparkles shine so bright.
Nature wakes with soft delight,
Whispers greet the new daylight.

Birds begin their sweet refrain,
A melody, not in vain.
Sunrise paints the hills in gold,
A story of warmth, retold.

Dewdrops glisten on the grass,
Each moment, time seems to pass.
Fresh begins the day anew,
In the sky, a palette blue.

Clouds drift slowly, soft and white,
The world awakes, pure and bright.
Every shadow gently fades,
In dawn's glow, the magic invades.

Hope unfurls with every ray,
Chasing dreams that softly sway.
In that crystal glow, we find,
A promise for the heart and mind.

# Light's Winter Embrace

Blankets white upon the ground,
Silent beauty all around.
Twinkling stars begin to fade,
As the dawn's light is displayed.

Branches lace with frosty sheen,
Nature's artwork, pure and clean.
Every breath a misty sigh,
Whispers softly by and by.

Children laugh in playful cheer,
Snowflakes dance and disappear.
In this wonder, hearts ignite,
Wrapped in warmth, a pure delight.

Candles flicker, glow so warm,
Cocooned safe from winter's charm.
Echoes of the hearth's embrace,
Finding joy in this still space.

Let us cherish moments shared,
In the warmth, we love declared.
Light's embrace in winter's chill,
Holds us close, our hearts to fill.

## Frosted Memories

Time stands still in frosted air,
Moments linger, pure and rare.
Frozen whispers, a quiet song,
Collecting threads where we belong.

Pictures framed in icy haze,
Reflecting on our golden days.
Every laugh and every tear,
Frozen echoes, crystal clear.

Beneath the layers, warmth survives,
In the dust of all our lives.
Every memory a star,
Guiding us from near to far.

Embers glow in every heart,
Frosty breath, a work of art.
Holding tightly to the past,
In these moments, love will last.

The chill may bite, the winds may blow,
Yet in memories, warmth will grow.
Frosted tales of days gone by,
Dance like feathers in the sky.

# Luminous Nightfall

As daylight wanes to twilight's tune,
Stars unveil their silver boon.
The moon climbs high, a beacon bright,
Casting dreams in softest light.

The world transforms in shades of blue,
Where shadows linger, hopes renew.
In the hush, a magic stirs,
While the vibrant night occurs.

Whispers travel on the breeze,
Carrying secrets through the trees.
Every sound a soothing balm,
The night wraps all in quiet calm.

Flickering flames in distant sight,
Drawing hearts to share the night.
Every flicker tells a tale,
In the dark where dreams prevail.

Hold this moment, breathe it in,
Embrace the peace that lies within.
Luminous night, a gentle song,
In your arms, we all belong.

# Serene Chill

A whisper drifts upon the air,
The world is wrapped in quiet care.
Soft snowflakes dance, a gentle fall,
In nature's hush, we hear it call.

Trees wear coats of frosted white,
Bathed in the soft, ethereal light.
The stars above, they twinkle bright,
In this serene and tranquil night.

The moon, a guardian on high,
Watches over as time slips by.
Each breath we take a plume of smoke,
In this stillness, our hearts awoke.

Footsteps crunch on crisp, cold ground,
In this quietude, peace is found.
With every step, the world feels new,
A canvas blank, in vibrant hue.

As dawn approaches, skies turn pink,
In this frozen world, we find the link.
To moments sweet, to hearts so true,
Serene chill, we cherish you.

# An Ice-Covered Dawn

Morning breaks with a silver gleam,
In every corner, a sparkling dream.
The world awakens, dressed in ice,
Each branch and blade, a crystal slice.

Sunlight streams through frosty trees,
A gentle kiss, a softening breeze.
The colors dance, the shadows play,
As night reluctantly gives way.

Birds alight in the golden glow,
Their songs arise, then softly flow.
In this waking, we see the art,
Nature's magic, a brand new start.

The icy coating, a tender shield,
Promises warmth from time's vast field.
In this moment, we stand as one,
Embracing all that has begun.

With each ray, the heart does soar,
This ice-covered dawn, we all adore.
A tranquil breath, a whispered sigh,
In this beauty, we learn to fly.

# Snowbound Radiance

Beneath a blanket, pure and white,
The world sleeps soundly, a wondrous sight.
Snowflakes glisten in morning's light,
Each one unique, a delicate flight.

Mountains rise in majestic grace,
Their peaks adorned, a frozen lace.
With every drift, our spirits lift,
In winter's embrace, a gentle gift.

Footprints lead through a snowswept trail,
In soft white whispers, we hear a tale.
Of laughter shared and dreams to chase,
In this snowbound, radiant place.

Children play in a flurry of joy,
Creating worlds with each little toy.
Snowmen stand with hats so wide,
Their jovial forms in the cold abide.

As day gives way to twilight's charm,
The night unfurls with a peaceful calm.
In the distance, a fireside glow,
Snowbound radiance, forever aglow.

## The Glow of Winter

In winter's grasp, a magic stirs,
With every breath, the silence purrs.
Frosted fields, a gentle hue,
The glow of winter, pure and true.

Candles flicker in twilight's glow,
Casting warmth through the fresh-fallen snow.
A tapestry spun with silver and gold,
Tales of wonder, quietly told.

The nights are long, the days are brief,
Yet in the chill, we find belief.
In every star that fills the night,
The glow of winter shines so bright.

We gather close, beneath the skies,
With steaming mugs, and gleaming eyes.
Stories shared, the fire's dance,
In this moment, we find our chance.

As seasons meld and time does flow,
We hold the glow, we let it grow.
For in winter's heart, we find the sun,
A gentle light, for everyone.

# Icy Starlight

In the night where stars collide,
Whispers dance on frosty air.
Moonlight glimmers, gentle guide,
Casting dreams beyond compare.

Snowflakes twirl, a silent flight,
Painting shadows on the ground.
Each one glistens, pure and bright,
A universe where hope is found.

Beneath the heavens, quiet grace,
Time stands still in winter's hold.
Each star wears a perfect face,
Tales of wonder yet untold.

Through the chill, our spirits soar,
Hearts entwined in icy bliss.
Every heartbeat, we explore,
In this moment, love's sweet kiss.

As dawn whispers its golden tune,
The world awakens, soft and slow.
But I will cherish this bright boon,
Forever held in starlit glow.

# Dazzling Silence

Amidst the noise, a hush unfurls,
A gentle breeze, the world holds still.
In this calm, our dreams can swirl,
Painted soft, a tranquil thrill.

Eyes closed tight, I hear the peace,
Nature's song, a soothing balm.
With every breath, I find release,
In silence deep, the heart feels calm.

Stars above in velvet skies,
Whispers passionate and low.
In dazzling silence, spirits rise,
Echoing the love we know.

Each moment glistens like a dream,
A tapestry of thoughts entwined.
In this quiet, we redeem,
Lost connections, hearts aligned.

As day breaks, still shadows play,
But in my heart, the night stays near.
Dazzling silence, a sweet ballet,
In memories, forever clear.

# Frost-edged Ruins

Amidst the stones, the past lies bare,
Frosted edges, whispering tales.
Echoes linger in the air,
Time has woven fragile trails.

Nature's grip on ancient walls,
Silent stories, etched in ice.
In the stillness, twilight calls,
Beauty finds its sacrifice.

Covering shards of what once gleamed,
Winter's breath whispers as it flows.
In these ruins, dreams are dreamed,
While the chill of history grows.

With every step, the echoes guide,
Lost in time's enigmatic dance.
Frost-edged secrets, where shadows bide,
Inviting souls to take a chance.

Through crumbling paths, the heart shall roam,
In icy silence, we hold dear.
Ruins echo, yet feel like home,
Reminding us that love is here.

# Twilight's Crystal Cloak

As day dissolves, the light concedes,
Twilight wraps the world in grace.
In soft hues, the heart then pleads,
For moments treasured in this space.

The sky wears shades of deepening blue,
Each star ignites, a spark divine.
In the glow, our shadows grew,
Wrapped in magic, pure and fine.

With every breath, the night unfolds,
A crystal cloak of dreams untold.
Beneath this sky, our love beholds,
Promises whispered, soft and bold.

In this twilight, we dare to soar,
Hearts entwined, forever true.
Amongst the stars, we find our more,
In twilight's arms, I stand with you.

From dusk till dawn, we share this light,
In every moment, pure delight.
Twilight's crystal cloak shines bright,
Guiding souls to love's sweet height.

# Enchanted Snowlight

In the hush of a winter's night,
Snowflakes dance, pure and bright.
Whispers of magic fill the air,
Shimmering dreams linger everywhere.

Moonbeams cast a gentle glow,
On crystal branches, soft and slow.
The world transformed, a wonderland,
Where silence paints with a gentle hand.

Footprints crunch on frozen ground,
A symphony of peace resound.
In this realm of icy grace,
Every shadow finds its place.

Glistening layers blanket the earth,
Each flake a tale of rebirth.
Whirling twirls in the frosty breeze,
Nature's secrets, held with ease.

So let us wander, hand in hand,
Through this enchanted, snowy land.
In every moment, pure and bright,
We find our joy in snowlight's sight.

# Celestial Chill

Stars ignite in a velvet sky,
Whispers of winter's lullaby.
A breath of frost, a fleeting thrill,
Underneath the celestial chill.

The air is crisp, the silence profound,
Nature's magic softly surrounds.
Twinkling lights in the distance gleam,
In this frosty world, we dare to dream.

Crystalline branches, adorned with grace,
Holding the wonders of time and space.
Every flicker tells a tale,
Of tranquil nights on a moonlit trail.

Breath as vapor in the frigid night,
Creating art with pure delight.
Wrapped in warmth, the stars we chase,
In the heart of this icy embrace.

So let the world spin, come what may,
With you beside me, I'll find my way.
In every heartbeat, a thrill to fill,
Our spirits dancing in the celestial chill.

# Glistening Silence

Upon the ground, a blanket lies,
Glistening soft beneath the skies.
The world adorned in a sparkling veil,
Where every whisper tells a tale.

Stillness reigns, yet life abounds,
In hidden corners, beauty surrounds.
A moment frozen, forever bright,
In the tender glow of soft twilight.

Gentle flakes, in silence, fall,
Nature's wonder, captivating all.
In the cold, we find our peace,
As time slows down, our worries cease.

Echoes linger in the frosty air,
In each breath, a promise to share.
The glistening world, wrapped in white,
Holds secrets whispered in the night.

So let us savor every glance,
In this glistening silence, we chance.
Together exploring, side by side,
In the heart of winter, our joy will abide.

# Frosted Echoes

In the quiet of dawn's embrace,
Frosted echoes leave their trace.
Nature's canvas painted white,
Awakens dreams in morning light.

Every twig, a crystal art,
Whispers of winter touch the heart.
As sunlight kisses icy ground,
A symphony of beauty found.

Footsteps carve through shimmering dew,
In frosted fields, a world anew.
Each breath a cloud in the chill of air,
Memories woven with tender care.

The laughter of children, twinkling eyes,
In this wonder, spirits rise.
Snowflakes twirl in a playful dance,
Wrapped in the joy of winter's romance.

So hold my hand, let's wander wide,
Through frosted echoes, side by side.
In every moment, let love be our guide,
In the beauty of winter, our hearts open wide.

# Frost-laden Twilight

The twilight glows with icy breath,
Shadows creep where warmth was left.
Trees stand still, their limbs adorned,
In silence deep, the night's reborn.

Stars like diamonds, distant, bright,
Whisper secrets of the night.
Each flake dances in the air,
A fleeting moment, pure and rare.

Moonlight bathes the world in white,
Chilling hearts, yet feelings light.
Nature's brush paints every scene,
A winter wonder, soft and serene.

Footsteps crunch on frosty ground,
Echoes linger all around.
In the stillness, dreams take flight,
In the magic of this night.

Hold your breath, the world's aglow,
In frosted dreams, let your heart go.
Twilight whispers, softly calls,
In the cold, where beauty falls.

# Dusting of Magic

A light dusting on the earth,
Whispers of an unseen birth.
Every grain, a tale unfolds,
In the quiet, mystery holds.

Sparkling under morning sun,
Each glimmering flake, a run.
Magic swirls in every breath,
Painting life, defying death.

The world awakes in shimm'ring light,
Colors merge, dark turns bright.
Fairy tales through shadows creep,
In this wonder, secrets keep.

Children laugh, their joy unbound,
With every step, enchantment found.
Snowflakes twirl in playful streams,
Glimmers of our wildest dreams.

Hold the magic in your heart,
Feel the wonder, take your part.
In this dusting of delight,
Find your joy, embrace the night.

# Glistening Resilience

Through winter's chill, the flowers fight,
Beneath the frost, they cling to light.
A glistening hope in frozen ground,
Their quiet strength, a beauty found.

Branches bend but do not break,
Ice and snow, the paths they take.
Each morning's light, a fresh new chance,
Nature's hand, a steadfast dance.

Resilience found in every leaf,
A promise held beyond belief.
Through storms that lash and winds that wail,
The heart beats strong, it will prevail.

In glistening fields, new life will soar,
Breaking through and seeking more.
With every dawn, the cycle spins,
A tale of strength, where life begins.

Embrace the frost, the cold's caress,
For in the struggle, we find our best.
Glistening dreams through the darkest night,
In resilience, we find our light.

## Dreamscape in Ice

In a dreamscape spun of ice,
Silent worlds that feel so nice.
Mountains tall with peaks so proud,
Wrapped in silence, in a shroud.

Reflections dance on frozen streams,
Shadows weave through whispered dreams.
Every glimmer, a tale to tell,
In this magic, hearts compel.

Frosted echoes of the past,
Moments cherished, memories cast.
In the stillness, visions bright,
Guide us through the velvet night.

Wander through this icy land,
With each step, you understand.
Dreams unfold in blankets white,
Cradled in the tranquil night.

Awake your spirit, let it glide,
In this dreamscape, magic hides.
Life and beauty intertwined,
In ice-bound realms, the heart aligned.

# Whispering Ice Light

In the stillness of the night,
Whispers dance with ice light,
Crystals gleam beneath the moon,
Nature's breath, a quiet tune.

Branches glisten, diamonds glow,
Softly, cold winds begin to blow,
Silent echoes fill the air,
Magic woven everywhere.

Footsteps crunch on frosted ground,
In this realm, peace can be found,
Every flake a story told,
In the chill, a warmth unfolds.

Light will fade, but memories stay,
Of winter's charm, in shades of gray,
Each moment captured, fleeting, bright,
Lost in the dream of ice light.

As dawn approaches, colors bloom,
Soft hues dispel the night's gloom,
Yet in the heart, the frost remains,
Whispering tales of snowy chains.

# Shimmering Frosted Veil

Veils of frost embrace the morn,
Nature's cloak, ethereal, worn,
A world transformed in silver hue,
Every surface, a canvas new.

Sunrise casts its golden thread,
Through the mist, where dreams are bred,
Whispers of warmth begin to rise,
Underneath these frost-kissed skies.

Glistening trees dance in delight,
Cradling beams of pale sunlight,
In the quiet, life takes pause,
Respects the magic, loves the cause.

Footprints lead through fields of white,
Chasing shadows, pure and bright,
Each step a note in winter's song,
In this place, we all belong.

As day unfolds, the splendor fades,
Yet in our hearts, the beauty stays,
A frosted veil, a fleeting dream,
Of shimmering light, a sparkling stream.

## Soft Brilliance of Winter

Winter whispers soft and low,
A brilliance wrapped in serene glow,
Each flake a note in nature's rhyme,
Floating softly, lost in time.

Fires crackle with warmth and light,
Embers dance in the tranquil night,
While outside, the world is still,
Wrapped in frost, a silent thrill.

The air is crisp, breaths come out white,
Moments held in the soft twilight,
Every shadow, a tranquil prayer,
In winter's arms, we find our care.

Stars twinkle through the icy veil,
Telling stories, old and frail,
The moon watches with gentle eye,
As night deepens, the snowflakes sigh.

A landscape pure, a world so bright,
In the soft brilliance of the night,
Winter's beauty, a magic spun,
In every heart, it lives as one.

## Radiant Cold

In the grasp of winter's bold,
Lies a charm both fierce and cold,
Each breath a whisper, soft and clear,
Radiant dreams that draw us near.

Icicles hang like crystal spears,
Holding back the flow of years,
A fleeting moment, sharp and bright,
In the heart of winter's night.

The dance of snowflakes, pure and free,
Spins a tale for you and me,
Gentle drifts cover the ground,
In this silence, peace is found.

Footsteps lead to paths untold,
Through the beauty of radiant cold,
Echoes of laughter fill the air,
In the chill, a warmth we share.

As the horizon blushes pink,
In the cold, we dare to think,
Of moments cherished, hearts unfold,
In the embrace of radiant cold.

# A Symphony of Cold

The wind whispers low, a chilling breeze,
It dances through trees, with effortless ease.
Each note creates shadows upon the ground,
In nature's embrace, pure silence is found.

Beneath a pale sky, the world holds its breath,
As icy fingers trace the paths of death.
Yet beauty persists, in stillness it gleams,
A symphony crafted from frost-laden dreams.

The rivers lie still, their waters like glass,
Reflecting the stars, as the moments pass.
Quietly whispers the night to the day,
In harmony deep, the cold finds its way.

A twilight that shimmers with each frozen tear,
It cradles the earth, whispering near.
With each fleeting moment, the chill holds tight,
A symphony warming the heart of the night.

As dawn finally breaks, the music takes flight,
The chill of the cold gives way to the light.
Yet echoes remain, in the frost's soft glow,
A melody lingers, in the deep, quiet snow.

## Glimmer of Snow

In the hush of the morning, a glimmer appears,
A blanket of white, softening fears.
Each flake, a whisper, as delicate as lace,
Dances with joy, in a fragile embrace.

The world is transformed, a canvas so bright,
Underneath the sun's warm, golden light.
With laughter and play, the children arise,
Chasing the snowflakes that fall from the skies.

Each shimmering flurry, a tale of its own,
In the silence it brings, a beauty is known.
As footprints are left in the frosty expanse,
A moment of magic, a child's winter dance.

The pine trees are dressed in a silvery gown,
A glimmer of hope in the cold, darkened town.
As evening approaches, the snow starts to glow,
A dazzling display in the twilight's slow flow.

With peace in the night, the world seems to pause,
In the calm of the snowfall, we find our cause.
To cherish the beauty, in quiet we know,
The magic alive in the glimmer of snow.

# Illuminated Flakes

In the heart of the night, when all seems asleep,
Soft flakes start to fall, in silence they creep.
Each tiny particle, a star on the ground,
Illuminated wonders, where magic is found.

The moon casts its glow on the delicate snow,
Transforming the world, where soft whispers flow.
As shadows take shape in the silvery light,
The beauty of winter unfolds, pure and bright.

It twirls through the air, a ballet so sweet,
With every light touch, the earth feels the beat.
In unity dancing, in grace they align,
These illuminated flakes form a pattern divine.

The trees wear their coats, sparkling and bright,
Reflecting the luminescence of night.
As branches bow low, in reverence they bend,
To the artistry crafted, to the beauty we send.

With each frosty breath, the world starts to dream,
Of nights filled with wonder, where shadows gleam.
As dawn breaks the silence, the frost will be gone,
Yet the memory lingers, till the next winter's dawn.

# The Glow of Evening Frost

As twilight descends, with a whispering chill,
The world wraps in silence, a moment to fill.
The glow of the frost, like diamonds it beams,
Adorning the night with its delicate dreams.

Beneath the cool stars, the landscape aglow,
Each breath leaves a shimmer, a soft misty show.
The pathways are glistening, adorned in their best,
A canvas of crystals where nature can rest.

The branches hold treasures, like jewels on a tree,
Sparkling and twinkling, a sight to see.
As shadows stretch longer, the night plays its part,
In the glow of the frost, there's warmth in the heart.

And as evening deepens, the hush becomes thick,
Time slows down softly, like a magical trick.
The frost's gentle touch will cradle the ground,
In the embrace of the night, pure beauty is found.

With dreams in the air, a serenity's cost,
We cherish the stillness, despite what is lost.
For the glow of the evening, so tenderly cast,
Holds moments of magic, eternally vast.

# The Glare of Ice

Beneath the moon's soft gaze, it shines,
A world of crystals, sharp designs.
Each step a whisper, careful, slow,
In shimmering silence, we wander, glow.

A single breath, the air so clear,
Frosted branches, nature's spear.
We move like shadows on the white,
In the glare of ice, hearts ignite.

The stars above twinkle in delight,
As we trace patterns, night's true light.
A dance of diamonds, pure and bright,
Cloaked in the beauty of winter's bite.

In every glimmer, stories told,
Of ancient secrets, brave and bold.
The cold embraces with a silent cheer,
A world transformed, all crystal clear.

So let us cherish this frozen scene,
Where time stands still, and hearts stay keen.
In every glance, a wondrous sight,
Together forever, in the glare of light.

## Cold Fireflies

In the stillness of a winter night,
Fireflies flicker, a ghostly light.
They dance through shadows, soft and low,
Whispers of warmth in the frost's glow.

Each tiny spark, a story we share,
Cold yet comforting, floating in air.
In every flutter, a promise shines,
Amidst the chill, magic aligns.

Glistening trails in the velvet dark,
Guiding our way with a gentle spark.
We chase the dreams that come alive,
In the embrace of cold, we thrive.

Though winter's breath brings a biting chill,
These flickers of hope, they thrill and fill.
With laughter and warmth, we come together,
Cold fireflies shining, despite the weather.

So let our spirits dance and soar,
As winter whispers, we long for more.
In every moment, a light can spark,
Turning the cold into a warm remark.

## Flickering Frost

Morning breaks with a silver hue,
Frosted breath, the world anew.
Each blade of grass, a jeweled sight,
Whispers of winter, pure delight.

Flickers of sunlight through icy trees,
Gentle warmth carried on the breeze.
Nature's canvas, painted white,
In the stillness, hearts take flight.

Every crystal, a moment caught,
A fleeting memory, cherished thought.
In the crisp air, laughter rings,
Under the beauty that winter brings.

Treading softly, we leave our trace,
In this wonderland, a tender space.
The frost may fade, the day will grow,
But memories linger in the afterglow.

So let us bask in the frosty grace,
Embrace the chill, life's warm embrace.
For flickering frost holds secrets deep,
In its fleeting beauty, promises sleep.

# Kisses from Winter's Heart

With every flake that falls from sky,
Winter's breath, a gentle sigh.
Frosty kisses on cheeks so warm,
A loving touch, a soft, sweet charm.

Blankets of white, the earth adorned,
In silent wonder, hearts are warmed.
Every whisper of the chilly air,
A tender promise, love laid bare.

In the stillness, our souls unite,
Guided by stars, our hearts take flight.
The world transforms with each soft kiss,
In winter's heart, we find true bliss.

Through icy paths, we wander wide,
Hand in hand, we take each stride.
The cold may bite, but we are bold,
Finding warmth in the tales retold.

So let the winter's spirit flow,
Embrace the chill, let our love grow.
For kisses from winter's heart will stay,
In every moment, come what may.

# Glacial Glisten

Icebergs float on blue seas,
Shimmering like jewels bright.
Reflecting the sun's warm ease,
Nature's perfect, frozen light.

Cascades of frost gently fall,
Whispering secrets to the night.
Crystals sparkle, standing tall,
In the quiet, pure delight.

A chill wraps around the land,
With each breath, a misty sigh.
In this wonderland so grand,
Dreams ignite and softly fly.

Beneath the sky, a glacial dome,
Where silence reigns, and hearts feel free.
In this place that feels like home,
All worries fade into the sea.

Embrace the serene, the still,
Of glacial glimmers, shining true.
In nature's peace, we find our will,
A world reborn in icy hue.

## Snowy Radiance

Gentle flakes of white cascade,
Blanketing the earth with grace.
A silent beauty, unafraid,
Transforming each familiar place.

In the luminous moonlight glow,
Snowy radiance softly gleams.
Every corner starts to show,
A winter's dream with whispered dreams.

Footprints print the pure white quilt,
Stories told with each delight.
Layers of magic deftly built,
Crafting shadows in the night.

Trees adorned with frosted crowns,
Sparkling in the early dawn.
Nature wears her royal gowns,
In this serene, snowy yawn.

Let hearts dance in this pure light,
Feel the wonder, soft and bright.
In this snowy world, take flight,
As dreams drift gently out of sight.

## Twilight's Frozen Gleam

As day gives way to night's embrace,
Twilight's hues begin to blend.
A frozen gleam, a fleeting grace,
Where shadows stretch and softly mend.

Stars awaken in the sky,
Whispers of cold, inviting dreams.
In this hour, time seems to fly,
With every glimmer, hope redeems.

Winter's breath hangs in the air,
Painting silver on the ground.
In this moment, free from care,
Peaceful stillness, all around.

Night blooms with a crystalline spark,
Each twinkling light a soft caress.
In the silence after dark,
Serenity, our hearts confess.

Let us treasure this calm scene,
As twilight wraps the world in dreams.
In nature's arms, we drift serene,
With love and peace, our spirits beam.

# Celestial Frost

Underneath the starry dome,
Celestial frost begins to rise.
Crystals weave and dance like foam,
Painting magic across the skies.

In the depth of night it gleams,
A tapestry of light and shade.
In the quiet, hope redeems,
As nature's chill whispers, unafraid.

Gentle winds caress the trees,
Each branch adorned in icy lace.
The world awakens with a breeze,
Carving beauty in time and space.

As dawn approaches, softly glows,
Frosted leaves begin to twirl.
In each crystal, a story flows,
Reflecting shades that dance and whirl.

Forever in this cosmic dance,
Celestial frost, a fleeting gleam.
In every wonder, we find chance,
To chase the magic, live the dream.

## Cold Dance of Light

In the twilight's gentle embrace,
Shadows twirl in icy space.
Stars flicker in the chilly night,
An echo of the fading light.

Whispers float on winter's breath,
A graceful waltz, an art of death.
Crystal dreams in silence weave,
Moments lost, but hearts believe.

The moon casts silver beams so shy,
Over frozen streams they lie.
In this dance where silence reigns,
Nature's song through frost remains.

Glimmers spark in frosty air,
Tender beauty, cold yet rare.
Echoes of a brightened dawn,
In the cold, our hopes are drawn.

## Petals of Ice

Frosted blooms in winter's chill,
Delicate, yet strong of will.
Petals glisten, every hue,
Nature's art, a wintry view.

Brittle leaves on quiet ground,
In their beauty, peace is found.
A soft crunch beneath my feet,
Nature's symphony, bittersweet.

Hues of blue and pale white grace,
Time stands still in this frozen place.
Each petal whispers secrets old,
A tale of warmth amidst the cold.

Ornaments on branches sway,
Frozen jewels in bright array.
Winter's touch in gentle lace,
Nature's heart, a warm embrace.

## Glittering Expanse

Wide, the world in crystals gleams,
Blanketing earth in frosty dreams.
Stars are scattered on the snow,
A glittering expanse, pure and slow.

Mountains wrapped in icy gowns,
Silent whispers through the towns.
Every flake a story told,
In the night, the secrets unfold.

Moonlight dances on the hills,
Creating magic, winter thrills.
Underneath the vast, dark sky,
Every breath a soft goodbye.

Snowflakes twirl, they kiss the ground,
As the wild wind twirls around.
In this beauty, hearts ignite,
In the stillness of the night.

# Frosty Mirage

In the distance, the shimmer shows,
A frosty landscape, beauty glows.
Mirages dance on shimmering lakes,
Nature plays, and silence wakes.

Crystal vistas stretch so wide,
Reflections hide where dreams abide.
Each soft ripple tells a tale,
A glistening story, cold yet frail.

Winter's breath in shadows deep,
Holding secrets that it keeps.
In this calm, the world stands still,
Embracing peace, a quiet thrill.

Frosted echoes in the air,
Carry whispers without a care.
Every moment like a sigh,
Capturing time as it floats by.

# The Silent Gleam

In the hush of night, whispers sigh,
Stars twinkle softly in a velvet sky.
Each glow a secret, a tale untold,
In the silent gleam, the world unfolds.

Moonbeams dance on the tranquil lake,
Reflecting dreams that shadows make.
A quiet promise in the cool breeze,
Carried gently through the swaying trees.

The stillness wraps like a warm embrace,
Time stands still in this sacred space.
Heartbeats echo in rhythm and rhyme,
In the silent gleam, we pause our climb.

With every flicker, a memory gleams,
Lost in the fabric of midnight dreams.
Each glimmer guides us on our way,
Through the calm of night, till break of day.

In the glow, there's solace to find,
A fleeting moment, a peace of mind.
As dawn approaches, the stars will wane,
Yet the silent gleam will still remain.

## Sparkling Shadows

Beneath the trees where whispers play,
Sparkling shadows come out to sway.
Each flicker dances, a fleeting glance,
In the twilight's soft, enchanting trance.

Golden hues in the fading light,
Illuminate the paths of night.
Silhouettes weave through the gentle dark,
As stars ignite, leaving their mark.

Mysteries linger where silence sleeps,
Every shadow secrets keeps.
Hushed laughter mingles with the air,
In sparkling shadows, dreams lay bare.

A soft embrace of night's cool breath,
Filling the heart as it flirts with death.
In these moments, the world feels right,
Lost in the glow of starry light.

Upon the dawn, the shadows fade,
Yet in our hearts, their magic stayed.
In every step, they leave their trace,
A dance of light, a timeless grace.

## Moonlit Frost

In the stillness of the midnight hour,
Crisp and cold like a hidden flower.
Moonlight glimmers on frozen ground,
In moonlit frost, magic is found.

Each breath a whisper, a soft silver mist,
Nature's beauty, too rare to resist.
Icicles hang like delicate art,
A winter's tale, a lover's heart.

Shadows stretch in the pale moonlight,
Entranced, we wander through the night.
Every step crunches, a melodic sound,
In moonlit frost, we lose, then are found.

Dew drops sparkle like diamonds bright,
Painting the landscape in shimmering white.
Underneath the celestial dome,
In this frozen world, we feel at home.

As dawn approaches, the frost may fade,
But memories linger, the night they made.
In our hearts will forever stay,
The magic of moonlit frost's ballet.

## Frigid Luminescence

Cold winds blow through the valley wide,
Frigid luminescence, nature's pride.
A glow ignites in the frosty air,
In icy realms, enchantment is there.

Each flake that falls, a whisper of light,
Wrapping the world in a cloak of night.
Glittering paths where the shadows creep,
In frigid luminescence, silence runs deep.

Crystals form on the branches bare,
Nature's artistry, beyond compare.
Every shimmer tells a story grand,
Of winter nights across the land.

Stars above mirror the frost below,
In a dazzling dance, a cosmic show.
In this chill, there's a warmth we find,
In frigid luminescence, hearts unwind.

As the sun rises, the magic will wane,
But the memories linger, sweet and plain.
In every heart, a spark will stay,
Of frigid beauty at close of day.

## Ethereal Icebound Glow

In the hush of twilight's grace,
A shimmering light finds its place.
Whispers of frost in the air,
Casting dreams without a care.

Stars above begin to weave,
Tales of wonder we believe.
A world draped in crystal sheen,
Awakens magic, still unseen.

Frozen rivers softly sigh,
Reflecting colors from the sky.
Each flake falls like whispered hopes,
In this realm, the spirit copes.

Beneath the boughs of silvered trees,
The wind sings softly through the leaves.
A dance of shadows, light's embrace,
In the glow of this frozen place.

Ethereal dreams begin to flow,
In this winter's wondrous glow.
With every breath, a story spun,
Of icebound magic, we are one.

## Twinkling Frosted Horizons

Across the fields, a crystal sheet,
Where frosted whispers softly greet.
Horizons glisten, bright and clear,
A twinkling world, devoid of fear.

Snowflakes dance in playful flight,
Beneath the glow of soft moonlight.
Each shimmer tells a tale so sweet,
Of winter's charm in every beat.

In the distance, mountains rise,
Veiled in white beneath the skies.
A spectacle of grand design,
Where earth and heaven intertwine.

With every dawn, the magic glows,
In frost-kissed mornings, beauty grows.
Colors burst as day awakes,
Painting joy with every flake.

Twinkling frost, a canvas bright,
Crafting dreams in soft twilight.
In this world, wonder ignites,
As nature's spark begins its flights.

# Frost's Gentle Caress

A soft embrace from winter's hand,
Enchanting every barren land.
Frosty fingers trace the night,
Whispering secrets, pure delight.

Each blade of grass a jeweled plume,
In nature's quiet, gentle bloom.
With every touch, a hushed refrain,
Frost's caress, a sweet campaign.

Underneath the silver sky,
The world feels still, a muted sigh.
A blanket of white, so pure, so light,
Wraps the earth in love's soft sight.

As moonbeams dance on frozen streams,
Frost weaves softly through our dreams.
In this calm, our hearts entwine,
With nature's breath, all becomes fine.

Frost's gentle touch, a loving sign,
Inviting us to pause, align.
In silence, let the magic flow,
In warmth of heart, we greet the snow.

# Winter's Glint

Winter's sheen on every face,
Sparkling softly in its grace.
Glints of silver, crisp and bright,
Illuminating the cold night.

The air is filled with frosty cheer,
As laughter spreads, so warm and near.
In every flake, a story told,
Of winter's charm, both shy and bold.

Candles flicker, shadows play,
In cozy nooks where hearts will stay.
Hot cocoa warms our chilly hands,
As winter's magic slowly stands.

Beneath the stars, we find our way,
In whispered dreams, we gladly sway.
In every glint, a moment found,
Of union sweet with love unbound.

Winter's glow, a gentle balm,
Wrapping us up in soothing calm.
In every heartbeat, winter sings,
Of hope that only cold wind brings.

www.ingramcontent.com/pod-product-compliance
Ingram Content Group UK Ltd.
Pitfield, Milton Keynes, MK11 3LW, UK
UKHW031945151224
452382UK00006B/88